Bon to you dear

Peter

Hugo

P

2011

GUIDE TO LIFE

GUIDE TO LIFE

RUNNING PRESS
PHILADELPHIA · LONDON

Family Guy ™ & © 2011
Twentieth Century Fox Film Corporation.
All rights reserved.
Published by Running Press, A Member of the
Perseus Books Group

Books published by Running Press are available
at special discounts for bulk purchases in the United
States by corporations, institutions, and other
organizations. For more information, please contact
the Special Markets Department at the Perseus
Books Group, 2300 Chestnut Street, Suite 200,
Philadelphia, PA 19103, or call (800) 810-4145, ext.
5000, or e-mail special.markets@perseusbooks.com.

ISBN 978-0-7624-4306-2
Library of Congress Control Number: 2011923420

9 8 7 6 5 4 3 2 1
Digit on the right indicates the number of this printing

Designed by Jason Kayser
Edited by Cindy De La Hoz
Typography: American Typewriter, Candice, and
Garage Gothic

Running Press Book Publishers
2300 Chestnut Street
Philadelphia, PA 19103-4371

Visit us on the web!
www.runningpress.com

INTRODUCTION

Since its debut in 1999, *Family Guy* has been an unfailing source of subversive hilarity, and the Griffins have become part of our extended family. There's Peter, the lovable oaf who doesn't hesitate to speak his mind. His wife, Lois, is the voice of reason; one-year-old Stewie, the voice of doom. There's sweet-hearted son Chris and daughter Meg, the eternal outsider. Brian the dog, of course, is a true gentleman with an answer for everything and a martini for every occasion. Cleveland Brown, Glenn Quagmire, and Joe Swanson help keep things light and the beer suds flowing. What wonderful memories!

If you look closely, you can see how everything you need to know to make it in this world can be learned by watching the eclectic family from Quahog and their friends. So, dear reader, sit back and prepare for a trip down memory lane with some of the greatest *Family Guy* moments and a load of wicked sweet Griffin-style wisdom.

Stewie:

"Hello, mother.
I come bearing a gift.
I'll give you a
hint. It's in my
diaper and
it's not a toaster."

Stewie: "You ever heard of the multiverse theory, Brian?"

Brian: "Of course I have—but I'm wondering if you have."

Stewie: "Oh my God, so transparent. The theory states that there are an infinite amount of universes coexisted with ours on parallel dimensional planes."

Brian: "The dimensional planes, right."

Stewie: "Oh, don't do that. Don't repeat the last two words like you already kind of knew what I was talking about. You have no idea what I'm talking about."

THE ART OF SUBTLETY:

Lois:

"SHUT UP AND LET'S DO IT."

Stewie:

"There's always been
a lot of tension between
Lois and me. And it's
not so much that I want to
kill her. It's just . . .
I want her not
to be alive anymore."

Quagmire:
"I did gagoogity
that girl. I gashmoigitied
her gaflavity with
my googis.
And I am sorry."

Peter:

"Okay, okay, wait, here's another one. Why do women have boobs? . . . So you got something to look at while you're talking to them."

Cleveland:
"All he needs is another lemon snow cone."

Peter:
"No thanks, that yellow snow cone you gave me didn't taste like lemon, it tasted more like . . . Oh, you guys are asses!"

Brian:

"How about a little less questions and a little more shut the hell up?"

Brian:

"I'M NOT DRUNK!

I JUST HAVE A SPEECH IMPEDIMENT."

Little Girl:
"Ewww!
Your breath
smells like kitty
litter!"

Stewie:
"I was curious!"

Stewie:

"I DON'T NEED TO $@%# IMPRESS YOU."

Peter:
"I'm a bad father, a lousy husband, and a snappy dresser."

Stewie:

"When the world is mine, your death shall be quick and painless."

Lois:

"My daughter needs a makeover like there's no freakin' tomorrow."

Chris:

"PERMISSION TO FREAK OUT?"

WATCH YOUR TEMPER:

Stewie:

"DAMN YOU AND SUCH!"

Peter:

"Ok, here's another riddle: a woman has two children. A homicidal murderer tells her she can only keep one. Which one does she let him kill?"

Lois:

"That's . . . that's not a riddle. That's . . . that's just terrible."

Peter:

"Wrong, the ugly one!"

Karina:

"Um, I'm new in town and I'm awfully lonely. I'm wondering if you wouldn't mind buying me a drink."

Brian:

"Well, that'd be my pleasure. And maybe later I can show you some of the local points of interest. There's one right below the table."

Lois:

"I'm going through
a phase . . .
where I'm only
attracted to
handsome men."

ALWAYS HAVE A SCAPEGOAT AVAILABLE:

Chris:

"OH, NO! SOMEONE PEED IN MY PANTS!"

Lois:

"It's like I always tell the kids, a quitter never wins and don't trust whitey."

Peter:

"Gays don't vomit. They're a very clean people. And they have been ever since they came to this country from France."

Stewie:

"I should be more reluctant to take my clothes off . . ."

CONFORMITY CAN BE BLISS:

Meg:

"I'M JUST TRYING TO FIT IN!"

WHY IT'S BEST NOT TO OVERTHINK THINGS:

Peter:

"I've got an idea— an idea so smart that my head would explode if I even began to know what I'm talking about."

Stewie: **"If I choose to make stool in my pants right now, you're the only one here to change me. What do you think of that, hmm?"**

Brian: **"I'm not going to change you."**

Stewie: **"What?"**

Brian: **"I said I'm not going to change you."**

Stewie: **"You can't be serious. . . . What if I make a fudgie? . . . Well, I just won't. I just won't, that's all. I just won't. Blast! I just did."**

THE ESSENTIALS OF GOOD PARENTING:

Lois:

"Peter! You're bribing your daughter with a car?"

Peter:

"Ah, c'mon, Lois. Isn't 'bribe' just another word for 'love'?"

Stewie:

"DAMN IT TO THE BLOODY BOWELS OF HELL!"

Peter:

"A boat's a boat but a box could be anything! It could even be a boat!"

Stewie:

"WHY YOU SICK, SICK LITTLE MOO COW!"

HOW TO GET OUT OF CHORES:

Peter: "I know something about stupid phone calls." [phone rings in house]

Lois: "Hello?"

Peter: "I can't take the trash out today. I'm working late at the office."

Lois: "The caller ID says you're calling from the kitchen. In fact, I can see you."

Peter: "Can you see me now?"

Lois: "No."

Peter: "Now I'm at the office."

Stewie:

"Forecast for tomorrow—a few sprinkles of genius with a chance of doom!"

Peter:

"Mr. Weed? This is Peter Griffin. I will not be coming to work today. I was in a terrible plane crash. My entire family was killed and I am a vegetable."

REMEMBER SOMETIMES IT'S JUST NOT WORTH THE TROUBLE:

Brian:

"Whose leg do I have to hump to get a dry martini around here?"

Brian:

"EXCUSE ME . . .
DO I
KNOW
YOU?"

HOW TO KEEP THE ROMANCE ALIVE:

Lois:

"Peter, I got a wax job and let's just say you're cleared for landing!"

Quagmire:

"You must be
a parking ticket,
'cause you
got fine written
all over you!"

THE IMPORTANCE OF LUBRICATION:

Greased-up Guy:

"YOU'RE NEVER GONNA CATCH ME!"

Stewie:
"I'm the dog. I'm well read and have a diverse stock portfolio. But I'm not above eating grass clippings and regurgitating them on the rug."

Brian:
"I'm a pompous little antichrist who will abandon my plans for world domination when I grow up and wind up settling with a rough trick named Jim."

Brian:

"If dogs aren't supposed to eat dental floss out of the trash, why did they make it mint flavored?"

Lois:
"You're drunk again."

Peter:
"No, I'm just exhausted because I've been up all night drinking."

Stewie:

"The outrages
I have suffered
today will
not soon
be forgotten!"

Peter:

"I had such a
crush on her—until
I met you, Lois.
You're my
silver medal."

Stewie:

"OBEY ME OR I'LL PUT YOU ON DIAPER DETAIL!"

Chris:

"THERE'S AN EVIL MONKEY IN MY CLOSET!"

Stewie:

"Ha! That's so funny I forgot to laugh— excluding that first 'Ha!'"

Peter:
"I don't take coupons from giant chickens, not after last time."

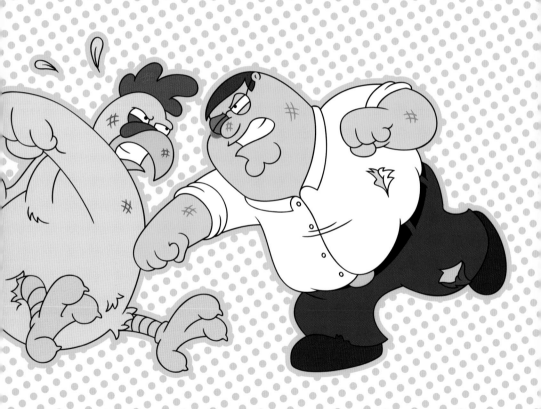

Stewie:
"Now, I'm going to do
something I like to call
the 'Compliment Sandwich,'
where I say something
good, talk about where you
need improvement,
and then end
with something good."

Quagmire:
"If I could change
the alphabet I
would put 'U' and 'I'
together."

Peter:

"What am I supposed to do with all my great ideas? Put them in a tub and clean myself with them? That's what soap is for."

Peter:

"LET'S GO DRINK 'TIL WE CAN'T FEEL FEELINGS ANYMORE!"

Peter: "I'm afraid I have some very bad news. Your wife's gonna be a vegetable. You're gonna have to bathe her, feed her, and care for her for the rest of your life."

Mr. Pewterschmidt: "Oh my God!"

Peter: "No no no. I'm just kidding. She's dead."

Quagmire:

"Hello, 911? It's Quagmire. Yeah, it's caught in the window this time."

Brian:
"I leave more personality in tightly coiled piles on the lawn."

Lois: "Why don't you go back
to that doctor and tell him to suck
the fat out of your head?"

Peter: "Maybe I will, and
then I'll put it on my feet and
skate on Paul Bunyan's
skillet to cook his flapjacks."

Lois: "That doesn't make any sense!"

Peter: "It doesn't have to,
Lois. I'm beautiful!"

Stewie:

"Let me guess, you picked out yet another colorful box with a crank that I'm expected to turn and turn until OOP! big shock, a jack pops out and you laugh and the kids laugh and the dog laughs and I die a little inside."

Stewie:

"Uh . . . you've reached Stewie
and Brian. We're not here
right now. . . . Uh, and if this
is mom, uh, send money because
we're college students and
we need money for books . . . and
highlighters . . . and . . .
ramen noodles . . . and condoms
for sexual relations with
our classmates."

Stewie:

"For God's sake, get off your ass and do some parenting!"

Peter: "I'LL BE **CHARLIE** AND YOU COULD ALL BE MY **ANGELS.**"

MEN SEEKING MAN

WANT A FOURSOME?
We need a fourth to round out our group. Already have a pilot, a cop, and a fat guy.
Contact: Peter Griffin